Dear Parents and Educators,

W9-BKK-065

Welcome to Penguin Young Readers! As parents and educators, you know that each child develops at his or her own pace—in terms of speech, critical thinking, and, of course, reading. Penguin Young Readers recognizes this fact. As a result, each Penguin Young Readers book is assigned a traditional easy-to-read level (1–4) as well as a Guided Reading Level (A–P). Both of these systems will help you choose the right book for your child. Please refer to the back of each book for specific leveling information. Penguin Young Readers features esteemed authors and illustrators, stories about favorite characters, fascinating nonfiction, and more!

Why Do Birds Sing?

LEVEL **3**

GUIDED
READING
LEVEL **L**

This book is perfect for a **Transitional Reader** who:
- can read multisyllable and compound words;
- can read words with prefixes and suffixes;
- is able to identify story elements (beginning, middle, end, plot, setting, characters, problem, solution); and
- can understand different points of view.

Here are some **activities** you can do during and after reading this book:
- Comprehension: After reading the book, answer the following questions.
  - Which bird can swim and dive?
  - Why does a hummingbird have a long beak?
  - What is a newborn bird called?
  - Why do some birds bathe in dust?
  - Which bird can sleep while flying?
- Labels: Some of the pictures in this book have labels. Go through the book and read the labels. What did you learn by reading the labels that you did not learn by reading the text? Next, find the pictures that do not have labels. Using the facts in the book, write labels—on sticky paper— and stick them on the appropriate pictures.

Remember, sharing the love of reading with a child is the best gift you can give!

—Bonnie Bader, EdM
  Penguin Young Readers program

*Penguin Young Readers are leveled by independent reviewers applying the standards developed by Irene Fountas and Gay Su Pinnell in *Matching Books to Readers: Using Leveled Books in Guided Reading*, Heinemann, 1999.

For Rena Bidwell, a wonderful neighbor—JH

For Remi and Brianna—AD

Penguin Young Readers
Published by the Penguin Group
Penguin Group (USA) Inc., 375 Hudson Street, New York, New York 10014, USA
Penguin Group (Canada), 90 Eglinton Avenue East, Suite 700, Toronto, Ontario M4P 2Y3, Canada
(a division of Pearson Penguin Canada Inc.)
Penguin Books Ltd, 80 Strand, London WC2R 0RL, England
Penguin Ireland, 25 St Stephen's Green, Dublin 2, Ireland (a division of Penguin Books Ltd)
Penguin Group (Australia), 707 Collins Street, Melbourne, Victoria 3008, Australia
(a division of Pearson Australia Group Pty Ltd)
Penguin Books India Pvt Ltd, 11 Community Centre, Panchsheel Park, New Delhi—110 017, India
Penguin Group (NZ), 67 Apollo Drive, Rosedale, Auckland 0632, New Zealand
(a division of Pearson New Zealand Ltd)
Penguin Books (South Africa), Rosebank Office Park, 181 Jan Smuts Avenue,
Parktown North 2193, South Africa
Penguin China, B7 Jiaming Center, 27 East Third Ring Road North,
Chaoyang District, Beijing 100020, China

Penguin Books Ltd, Registered Offices: 80 Strand, London WC2R 0RL, England

Text copyright © 2004 by Joan Holub. Illustrations copyright © 2004 by Anna DiVito. All rights reserved. First published in 2004 by Dial Books for Young Readers and Puffin Books, imprints of Penguin Group (USA) Inc. Published in 2013 by Penguin Young Readers, an imprint of Penguin Group (USA) Inc., 345 Hudson Street, New York, New York 10014. Manufactured in China.

Photo credits: Front cover, pages 1, 12, 14, 17 (parrot), 24–26, 29, 33–34, 41, 43, 45: © Dorling Kindersley; page 5: © Gail Shumway/Getty Images, Inc.; pages 6, 11, 21, 27: © Corel; page 7: © PhotoDisc Inc.; page 8: © Robert A. Tyrell Photography; pages 9, 15, 37: © PictureQuest; page 10: © Gay Bumgarner/Getty Images Inc.; page 17 (pelican): © National Geographic Image Collection; page 19: © Tom McHugh/ Photo Researchers Inc.; page 23: © Tom & Pat Leeson/Photo Researchers Inc.; page 28: © Fritz Prenzel; page 31: © W. Lynn Seldon Jr./Omni-Photo Communications, Inc.; page 35: © Digital Vision; page 39: © Getty Images, Inc.; page 40: © Paul McCormick/Getty Images, Inc.; page 48: © Dynamic Graphics.

Note: The information in this book is not complete and is not intended to provide professional advice regarding appropriate care, food, housing, toys, or games for your pet, or advice concerning the suitability of any of these pets for your family. Consult experts at your pet store, organizations that educate about birds, and your vet for more complete information about the pets in this book before purchasing these pets or any supplies for them. Always wash your hands before and after handling a bird or its cage. Birds may bite, scratch, carry disease, or provoke allergic reactions. Consult your doctor in the event of injury or allergic reaction. It is inadvisable to tame any wild birds to become pets. Review state, city, and local laws in your area before purchasing any bird, since it may be illegal to own some of the birds mentioned in this book in some locations.

The Library of Congress has catalogued the Dial edition
under the following Control Number: 2003064945

ISBN 978-0-14-240106-4

11

Why Do Birds Sing?

by Joan Holub

illustrated by Anna DiVito and with photographs

Penguin Young Readers
An Imprint of Penguin Group (USA) Inc.

Do you like birds?

Birds are interesting and fun to watch. Some birds are friendly and make great pets.

Popular pet birds include the parakeet, finch, parrot, canary, and cockatiel (say: KAHK-uh-teel).

Parrots

Black-Crowned Crane

How many different kinds of birds are there?

There are over 9,000 kinds of birds. Sparrows, robins, and pigeons are some well-known wild birds.

Birds live in cities, forests, marshlands, deserts, mountains, and everywhere else in the world.

Pigeon

Bee Hummingbird

What are the smallest and biggest birds?

The bee hummingbird weighs as little as a dime and lays eggs the size of peas!

An ostrich can grow up to nine feet tall and weigh 345 pounds! It lays 15 to 20 eggs at a time. Each egg is about seven inches long.

Ostrich

Why do birds have feathers?

Birds are the only animals with feathers. Feathers keep birds warm and dry and help them fly.

Some birds have feathers that are brightly colored to attract mates. A male bird's feathers are usually more colorful than a female's feathers.

Female Cardinal

Male Cardinal

Owl

Feathers with colors and patterns that look like the surrounding area help protect a bird by hiding it. This is called camouflage (say: CAM-o-flahj).

How do birds fly?

Birds have light, hollow bones and strong chest muscles.

The shape and movement of their feathered wings beating against the air help to lift birds. Once they are in the air, most birds must flap their wings to fly.

Parakeet

Some birds can glide, soar, or
hover when conditions are right.

An albatross can glide in the air
for hours without flapping its wings.

An eagle can soar on moving air
currents.

A hummingbird hovers in place
by moving its wings about 70 times
every second!

Can all birds fly?

Most birds can fly. Some birds, such as chickens, can fly only a few feet at a time.

The great bustard is the heaviest bird that is able to fly. It weighs up to 42 pounds.

But not all birds fly. The ostrich, kiwi, and penguin are some birds that can't fly.

Kiwi

Can any birds swim?

Most birds can't swim. Geese, swans, and ducks are some birds that can.

Birds that swim usually have webbed feet that work like paddles. A penguin swims and dives with wings shaped like flippers.

Why do birds have beaks?

A bird uses its beak to get food, carry things, and protect itself. The shape of a bird's beak shows us what kind of food it eats.

A hummingbird uses its long beak like a straw to drink nectar from a flower.

Parrots have hook-shaped beaks
strong enough to crack
hard nuts and seeds.

A pelican's beak scoops
fish out of the water and holds
them in a special pouch.

Parrot

Bird beaks never stop growing.
A bird chews on hard objects, which
wears its beak down and keeps the
beak from getting too long.

Pelican

17

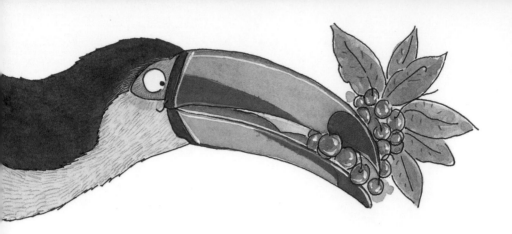

What do birds eat?

Birds may eat seeds, fruit, nuts, insects, fish, or small animals.

Woodpeckers drill holes into trees with their beaks and pull insects out with their long, sticky tongues.

Toucans use their beaks to pluck fruit from plants.

Owls eat small animals whole. Then they spit up a lump containing the animals' bones and fur.

Ivory-Billed
Woodpecker

How well do birds see?

Sight is a bird's most important sense.

A peregrine falcon can spot a mouse one mile away while flying very fast.

Penguins see very well in water, but not as well on land.

A bird's eyes are usually on the sides of its head. Each eye sees something different. This helps birds find food and avoid predators at the same time.

An owl's eyes face forward and are on the front of its head. Owls have to turn their heads around to look in other directions. Their large eyes let in lots of light, so they can see well at night.

Why do birds build nests?

Birds build nests to lay their eggs in and to protect their young.

A female bird usually builds the nest with twigs, sticks, moss, grass, or whatever she can find.

Some birds weave the pieces together. Others stick them together with mud. Nests are built in trees, barns, ponds, and in many other places.

One of the biggest nests was built by bald eagles in Florida. It was nine feet wide!

Not all birds make nests. Wild parrots lay eggs in holes they find in trees or in the ground.

Birds use their nests until their young can care for themselves.

How are
baby birds born?

All birds hatch from eggs laid
by a mother bird. One or both of
the parents sits on the eggs to keep
them warm until they are ready to
hatch. This warming time is called
incubation (say: enk-yu-BAY-shun).

The bigger a bird's egg is, the longer it usually incubates. An egg may incubate for as little as 10 days or as long as 80 days.

A male emperor penguin carries an egg on its feet for 65 days while it incubates.

Emperor Penguin

How do baby birds grow?

A newborn bird is called a chick. When they are born, most chicks don't have feathers and can't see. Their parents must bring them food and keep them warm.

Some parents swallow food, then bring it back to the nest and spit it up for their chicks to eat.

Most birds become fledglings (say: FLEJ-lings) when they are between

2 and 10 weeks old. This means they grow strong feathers and are ready to learn to fly.

Not all birds need help from their parents. The chicks born to chickens and some other birds can run around within a few hours of hatching!

Birds grow to full size within a year.

Blue Jays

How do birds take baths?

Many birds splash in shallow water to bathe. Some birds bathe in dust! This helps remove bugs from their feathers.

A bird also runs its beak through its feathers to comb, clean, and oil them. This is called preening.

Pet birds often try to preen their human owners' hair.

When do birds sleep?

Most birds sleep at night and take short naps during the day.

They may sleep standing up on one or both legs.

When a bird bends its knees, its toes lock tightly around a branch or perch so it won't fall off while it sleeps.

Wild birds sometimes sleep with one eye open to watch for danger.

Swifts can sleep while flying!

Owls and other nocturnal birds sleep during the day.

Flamingos

Why do birds sing?

Many birds sing to attract mates, tell other birds who they are, or warn enemies away. Male birds sing much more often than females do.

Most singing birds can't sing well unless other birds teach them when they are young. Chicks listen to their parents sing before trying it themselves.

Each type of bird sings a different song. Some types of birds can learn only one song.

Canaries keep adding new notes to their songs all their lives.

Mockingbirds can copy the songs of other birds.

Canary

Parakeets

Can birds really talk?

Many parrots and parakeets can repeat words or sounds they hear. They can't make up words, and must hear the same sound or word often before they learn to say it.

Some birds can copy the sound of a whistle, siren, or ringing phone.

To train a pet bird to talk, begin by repeating a single word several times a day. Practice when it's quiet and you are alone with your bird.

You might start by teaching your bird to say its name. After it learns that, you can slowly add more words.

Once a bird is able to speak its first word clearly, it will learn new words more easily.

Parrot

Are birds smart?

Most birds are smart. A pet bird may figure out how to unlatch its cage. It might learn to hop up a bird ladder or ring a bell.

People have taught their birds to play a simple game of tag.

Some parrots have been trained to play a short song on a piano or to ride a bird-size bike.

What jobs can birds do?

Homing pigeons can travel quickly over long distances and then return home again.

Ancient Greeks used pigeon messengers to send news about the Olympic Games.

A pigeon named Dear Friend received a medal for delivering important messages to an army in World War I. A written message was rolled up inside a tiny tube tied to the bird's leg with string.

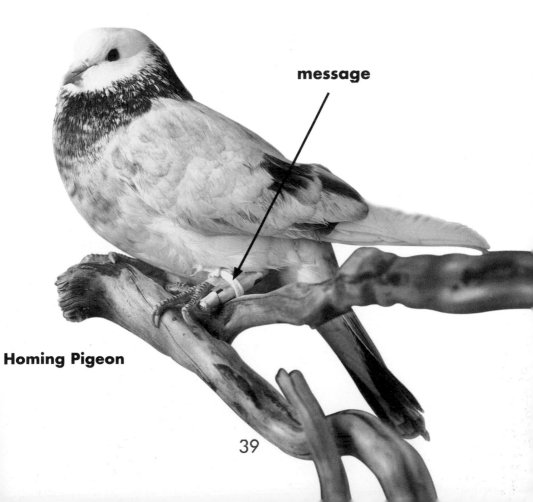

message

Homing Pigeon

Horned Puffins

Zebra Finches

Do birds like to be with other birds?

Birds can get lonely without other birds or people around. Parakeets, finches, and other birds may like to live in pairs or groups. Some birds want to be in a cage alone.

Many wild birds live together in groups called flocks. Pet birds sometimes think their owners are part of their flock.

Are pet birds easy to take care of?

Birds need food, water, shelter, friendship, and veterinary care.

Pet birds can be messy. They drop feathers, dust, and poop. Their cages must be cleaned often.

Birds need a cage with enough space to exercise their wings. Some pet birds like to be let out of their cages to fly in a large, safe area.

You should never leave a pet bird alone when it is out of its cage or let it fly freely outdoors. Get an adult's permission before releasing your bird.

Do birds like toys?

Pet birds need safe toys for fun
and exercise. Most birds like toys
they can hold and toys that dangle
or twirl. They also may like shiny,
colorful, or noisy toys. Many birds
will play on a swing or ladder.

Parakeets like to look at themselves in a mirror. They think they are seeing another bird.

Birds get bored with old toys and need a new toy now and then.

How can I make
a bird feeder?

You can turn a pinecone into
a bird feeder.

First, tie a string to the top of
a large pinecone. Spread peanut
butter all over the pinecone, then
roll it in birdseed until the peanut
butter is covered with seeds.

Hang your bird feeder on a tree branch outdoors. Watch from an inside window to see if birds visit your feeder!

Pet birds can be loving and playful. Each bird is a little different. Find out what your bird likes and needs. Be a good friend to your bird and it will be a good friend to you.